PRAYER THAT ACTUALLY WORKS!

By
Ryan Hicks
TaughtToProfit.com

Introduction

The basis of these prayers, and all prayer, is that the individual praying has faith in God that their prayer will be answered with a Yea and Amen. "For all the promises of God in him *are* yea, and in him Amen, unto the glory of God by us" (2 Corinthians 1:20). You may have times of doubt, but do not let these times cause you to venture off into double-mindedness or wavering, "For let not that man think that he shall receive any thing of the Lord" (James 1:7). The prayers given in this book are written in such a way that when you boldly decree them you will correspondingly build your faith for the thing you are decreeing.

> "Thou shalt also decree a thing, and it shall be established unto thee: and the light shall shine upon thy ways" (Job 22:28)

These prayers are not the typical begging, pleading, or whining to God for things that prayer has been relegated to by the masses of people who rarely get their prayers answered. These are bold prayers of strong faith in God and His unwavering willingness to bless you in all areas of your life. These are prayers where you are holding fast the profession of your faith without wavering, for He is faithful that promised (Hebrews 10:23). These are prayers that show forth that you are not trusting in uncertain riches, but in the living God, who gives you richly all things to enjoy (1 Timothy 6:17).

The most important aspect of praying these prayers is to make them part of your innermost being. You accomplish this glorious achievement by meditating on the specific prayer day and night, _and_ by taking action on them by decreeing the prayers multiple times a day. It is said of the blessed man mentioned in Psalm 1 that "whatsoever he doeth shall prosper" (Psalms 1:3). One of the key reasons for this prosperity in all areas was his practice of meditating day and night on the law of the Lord (Psalms 1:2). You too will take up this practice and meditate on these prayers day and night. This practice will only take you a few minutes a day, but you will soon see tangible results in your everyday life.

One of the fatal flaws in many people's prayers is that they really are doing less prayer and more begging, pleading, and daydreaming. Such people have no confidence in God's willingness to give them the desires of their hearts (compare that thinking with Psalms 37:4). They may also have limited confidence in God's ability to give them what they desire because they feel Satan and evil has more power to influence their daily lives than God. Few will voice that opinion because of how blasphemous it sounds, but their practice reveals this to be their underlying belief system. Even worse yet, some may truly believe that God is their enemy and is keeping them from blessings in order to "teach them a lesson" or other such excuse.

The most important part of prayer is that you first ask. Without asking, you will get nothing. This asking in not mere pleading or petitioning, but it goes further than that. It is your decreeing of these things in confident assurance that "no good _thing_ will he withhold from them that walk uprightly" (Psalms 84:11).

> "Hitherto have ye asked nothing in my name: ask, and ye shall receive, that your joy may be full." (John 16:24)

The simple promise is that if you ask, you shall receive. This is not a promise with numerous clauses and loopholes for God to get out of blessing you, as His desire is to give you all things. The hindrance to receiving is always on the receiver's part, not God's.

> "Ye lust, and have not: ye kill, and desire to have, and cannot obtain: ye fight and war, yet ye have not, because ye ask not. Ye ask, and receive not, because ye ask amiss, that ye may consume *it* upon your lusts." (James 4:2-3)

When you are asking for evil things and not the good things God freely gives, you are asking amiss, and will not receive. You cannot lust, kill, fight, and war, as mentioned in the previous verses in James, and expect God to lavish blessing upon you to aid you in your evil works.

> "Ask, and it shall be given you; seek, and ye shall find; knock, and it shall be opened unto you: For every one that asketh receiveth; and he that seeketh findeth; and to him that knocketh it shall be opened. Or what man is there of you, whom if his son ask bread, will he give him a stone? Or if he ask a fish, will he give him a serpent? If ye then, being evil, know how to give good

gifts unto your children, how much more shall your Father which is in heaven give good things to them that ask him?" (Matthew 7:7-11)

If we are honest with ourselves, we know that we have asked in prayer for things and have not received them. Knowing this, how can Jesus say that everyone who asks receives? The result is all in the way you ask. We are not asking in a faithless and beggarly way. Our asking is a bold declaration of the goodness of God Who is more willing to give good things to them that ask Him than the asker is to receive them.

"Why boastest thou thyself in mischief, O mighty man? the goodness of God *endureth* continually." (Psalms 52:1)

"Or despisest thou the riches of his goodness and forbearance and longsuffering; not knowing that the goodness of God leadeth thee to repentance?" (Romans 2:4)

"Behold therefore the goodness and severity of God: on them which fell, severity; but toward thee, goodness, if thou continue in *his* goodness: otherwise thou also shalt be cut off." (Romans 11:22)

Toward you God has only goodness, grace, and blessing. Once you understand God as Father, you can more easily grasp His goodness. Does any child expect their Father to give them a stone when they ask for bread? Why would we expect God to give us something bad when we ask for something good, or even worse yet, give us some new trial or suffering instead? The ideas of God being unwilling and capricious are not the teachings of Jesus, rather they are the teachings of faithless men trying to excuse their lack of results in life. For them it is easier to cast the blame on God and make themselves look spiritual for failing to receive from God.

> "Thus saith the LORD, the Holy One of Israel, and his Maker, Ask me of things to come concerning my sons, and concerning the work of my hands command ye me." (Isaiah 45:11)

This verse is so very objectionable to many religionists that new translations have even changed it from being a powerful statement about our unity with God to being an interrogation and sarcastic statement. They do this by adding an unwarranted question mark at the end of the verse, thus completely changing the powerful truth God gave to His children.

God gave man dominion on the earth and made him in the image and likeness of God (Genesis 1:27). As a child of God you have real power with God and He tells you that "concerning the work of my hands command ye me." This powerful truth reveals that we can hold God to His promises and "command" Him by commanding or decreeing the good things we desire.

This is not to be confused with usurping God's authority as Creator, rather it is to be understood as the child and Father relationship. In an earthly kingdom the word of a prince can have as much authority as the word of the king, if the king gives such authority to the prince. In the heavenly kingdom God placed His kingdom within us (Luke 17:21), made us partakers of the divine nature (2 Peter 1:4), and has given us the authority to decree things and see them established (Job 22:28). With this understanding we have no difficulty praying in full faith and confidence that we will get the thing we desired.

In Mark 11:24 Jesus promises, "Therefore I say unto you, What things soever ye desire, when ye pray, believe that ye receive *them,* and ye shall have *them.*" The fundamental principle that our Lord reveals here is that if we truly believe we have received that which we pray for, then we shall have them. What does this belief entail? Is it a mere mental acknowledgement of something we desperately hope will become true? No, for we all have prayed prayers that were more hope and less faith, and the end results were lacking. This belief is something deeper than mere mental assent. It includes holding to the thing desired as having been received presently **and** *feeling* as if we already have it. This would mean that praying to receive it again would be dissolving any faith we may have had in God when we first prayed, because if we truly believed that we received what things soever we desired *when we prayed* then we would not pray for them again and again and again. This is why we pray _once_ for the thing we desire and then we _decree_ the results desired as having already been received from that point onward.

Jesus uses the example of a child asking his father for bread (Matthew 7:7-11). After the child receives the bread would it be reasonable for him to keep pleading for bread? If he believes that he received the bread, then he would not continue to request it, for it is already his. This is the same way our prayers must be. We must originally ask for the things we desire in prayer, and then we confirm that we believed we have received by acting as if we have received them. Continuing to request the same thing over and over again only shows that we have not believed that we have received when we prayed. Since we have prayed in full faith we move on to feeling as if we have the thing desired.

Let me give an example of this faith in action. If your prayer was to travel to a foreign land, but you did not currently have the funds or time to do so, how would you exhibit the faith that you have believed you received? An act of faith that would prove you truly had believed that you received when you prayed would be to get your passport, get brochures for the location you will travel to, and make other plans necessary for your trip. There is nothing in your actual physical world that would cause you to do these things, but because you "walk by faith, not by sight" (2 Corinthians 5:7), you are acting by faith. You truly believe that you have received. To further improve your belief through your sub-conscience mind, you would visualize and *feel* getting on the plane, enjoying the flight, arriving in the country, enjoying the amenities you are looking forward to, and all the aspects of the trip you are desiring. The focus of the visualization is to feel the feelings you would have on the trip and all the experiences from it. You would then continue by faith to make the preparations for the trip, decree the desired result by faith, and visualize it happening, so that the only other thing to do besides these things is to wait for the answer to manifest in the physical world (Daniel 10:12-13).

Some of the prayers you may choose to pray for yourself may be hard for you to believe at first. This is where the meditating comes in. Meditation is an important determinant of whether you will get the desired result that you have believed for or if you will stop short and undo the blessing that is rightfully yours. I encourage you to modify them as needed in order to make them more personally applicable for your situation, but in doing so be careful to not diminish their strength or magnitude. Do not modify the prayer to make it weaker or "easier to believe." In the case of doubt, you shut the doubt down by doubling up your efforts meditating on the desired result having been received when you prayed.

Throughout your day make sure that you keep your thinking aligned with Philippians 4:8, which states:

> "Finally, brethren, whatsoever things are true, whatsoever things *are* honest, whatsoever things *are* just, whatsoever things *are* pure, whatsoever things *are* lovely, whatsoever things *are* of good report; if *there be* any virtue, and if *there be* any praise, think on these things."

What do you do if a negative thought arises which is contrary to the prayer of faith you have made? You follow 2 Corinthians 10:5, which states:

"Casting down imaginations, and every high thing that exalteth itself against the knowledge of God, and bringing into captivity every thought to the obedience of Christ."

As you decree these prayers multiple times a day you will start to make them part of you. The Scripture says of man, "as he thinketh in his heart, so *is* he" (Proverbs 23:7). This truth is one of the most powerful revelations we can have. Once you realize that your inner beliefs and who you really think you are is going to be what you *truly* are in life, you can then change that inner belief and get the results in life that you justly want.

I personally know how this inner belief can have a negative effect on your life. As a child, I grew up extremely poor. Everything in life was about lack, want, and struggle. When I got to be an adult and find great success and wealth, I would inevitably end up back in poverty, because that was who I really thought of myself as: the poor kid. In my heart, I was still that poor kid growing up lacking the things I desired and feeling less valuable than my middle-class friends. I thought in my heart that I was unworthy of wealth, riches, and success. Consequently, whenever I would find success and wealth in a business venture, I was always going to self-sabotage and end up back as "the poor kid."

None of this was done on purpose or consciously, of course. This was just my deep-rooted belief about myself and it created a self-image that I would always reflect back to the world. Instead of realizing my inner belief was at the root of the problem, I saw the inevitable failure and poverty as just a set of unfortunate circumstances, when the reality was that it was the direct result of my thinking. Until I changed that poverty mentality and renewed my mind to what and who I wanted to be, I would end back up at poverty every time. Once I thought in my heart that I was a successful and wealthy businessman, which I was, then things started to progress from glory to glory and from success to success.

The reality that whoever you think yourself to be is who you will be is why these prayers are so important. With these prayers you are praying in faith, believing that you received when you prayed, and then you turn the prayer into a declaration of that faith by decreeing it multiple times a day. This is done, not to convince God to grant the thing you desired, but to make you the person who is able to receive it. Instead of thinking in your heart of yourself as a sick person, you think of yourself as the healed and the whole of the Lord. Instead of thinking of yourself as a poor person, you think of yourself as the rich and successful person you really are. Instead of thinking of yourself as being a person who makes foolish decisions regularly, you think of yourself as the person endowed with great wisdom from their Creator. You create an image of yourself in your heart of the person you want to become, not the person you now are.

To summarize how to use the prayers in this book in one brief paragraph:

Believe that you have received whatever

you pray for when you pray. This means that you act as if you already have it and focus on feeling the way you would feel if you already had the answer right now by visualizing what you would do if the answered prayer were yours at the present moment. You then begin decreeing the prayer regularly, feeling and thinking as if you already received it.

QUESTIONS AND ANSWERS:

Q: Why are the prayers so short?

A: Jesus taught us to not use vain repetitions, as those who do this do so "for they think that they shall be heard for their much speaking" (Matthew 6:7). Long, drawn out prayers do not exhibit faith in God, but desperation and unbelief. Vain repetitions show a lack of faith in God, "for your Father knoweth what things ye have need of, before ye ask him" (Matthew 6:8). The purpose of prayer is not to convince God to come on your side and grant the petition of your heart, rather it is to align you fully in faith with His will for your good. This is why Jesus begins His statement about having "What things soever you desire, when ye pray" if you believe you receive them by saying, "Have faith in God" (Mark 11:22). Without faith in God's willingness to give you all things you will resort to long, drawn-out prayers and vain repetitions, because you are hoping that some of the great swelling of words will be the "magical" right combination of words that will get the desired result. Others believe their long prayer will pester God enough to convince Him to grant their request. God needs no convincing, you just need faith in Him.

Q: How long do I need to pray a specific prayer?

A: Since the prayers given in this book are more like faith-filled decrees, you can pray them as often and for as long as you want. They will not become vain repetitions because they are filled with praise for God's goodness and hearing of your prayer. They are confirmations of the result of your faith and are eternal representations that you have believed you received when you prayed (Mark 11:24). That having been established, when you have a "check" in your spirit that you no longer need to pray a certain prayer then your subconscious is convinced and the manifestation of the answered prayer is on the way. You could then choose to just pray the specific prayer once a week, as a memorial to the faithfulness of God in answering your prayer, and it also keeps your faith stirred up for the result continuing in your life.

Q: Why do I need to pray if God is willing my good already?

A: God's willingness to bless, prosper, heal, and enlighten you is never the issue. God "giveth to all life, and breath, and all things" (Acts 17:25), and your ability and/or willingness to receive is the issue. You are one of the most important beings that God has ever created. You were created in His image, after His likeness, and as such you have great untapped power with God and dominion on the earth (Genesis 1:26-27).

You are "called unto the fellowship of his Son Jesus Christ our Lord" (1 Corinthians 1:9). This fellowship or partnership is important to understand. God wants us to be partners with Him and He allows our choices, good or bad, in this life.

Q: How can I be sure of God's willingness to grant my request?

A: The promises of God are so complete for your every need that you can be certain He desires only your best. "For all the promises of God in him *are* yea, and in him Amen, unto the glory of God by us" (2 Corinthians 1:20). God's way of thinking and acting toward you is only goodness (Romans 11:22). A fundamental truth that is not understood by many is that "God is no respecter of persons" (Acts 10:34).

> "Thus saith the LORD, the Holy One of Israel, and his Maker, Ask me of things to come concerning my sons, and concerning the work of my hands command ye me." (Isaiah 45:11)

Q: Why is it not working for me?

A: Daniel could have felt this same way and given up on the 20th day after his petition, but then he would have stopped the angel who brought the answer by the 21st day (Daniel 10:12-13). All too often impatience stops people from receiving the blessing of God in their lives, but "let patience have *her* perfect work, that ye may be perfect and entire, wanting nothing" (James 1:4). I want to encourage you to remain in confident assurance that God has granted your request and "be not slothful, but followers of them who through faith and patience inherit the promises" (Hebrews 6:12).

> "What shall we then say to these things? If God *be* for us, who *can be* against us? He that spared not his own Son, but delivered him up for us all, <u>how shall he not with him also freely give us all things</u>?" (Romans 8:31-32)

Q: Why do I not see any evidence of the answer to my prayer?

A: You may be looking in all the wrong places. Your faith in and of itself is "the evidence of things not seen" (Hebrews 11:1). When you step out of faith to walk by sight, you terminate the results of your prayer, "For we walk by faith, not by sight" (2 Corinthians 5:7). It may also be that you are not taking note of the answer to your prayer. Oftentimes, we get in the mindset of our prayer having to be fulfilled in a certain specific way. This would mean that if you want a million dollars, God may have already answered, but you did not notice it because you were convinced that the money must come through a new job, when God may have given you an idea for a product that will benefit the world and sell by the millions. The Bible says of God that He "teacheth thee to profit, which leadeth thee by the way *that* thou shouldest go" (Isaiah 48:17). When you are meditating on your prayer be careful to listen to any thought, idea, or intuition that comes to mind. It would be wise to write these ideas down, regardless of whether they seem unrelated or random. If the idea to talk to a certain person keeps coming to mind, but it makes no sense in relation to your prayer, follow that leading of the Spirit. To ignore this leading is to choose to not receive the answer to your prayer.

Q: I want a person to do a certain thing, why is my prayer not working?

A: This is a fundamental error in the prayers of many people. They pray prayers of manipulation in order to get people to do their will, and then wonder why God is not granting their request. The way to pray for individuals is to pray for the character traits that you want them to be blessed with. So instead of praying, "I thank you God that my spouse does not yell at me or get angry easily," you would pray, "I thank you God that my spouse is calm, peaceful, and loving. I thank you that they are blessed with the fruit of the Spirit and righteousness, peace, and joy in the Holy Ghost."

This way of praying takes prayer from a place of trying to manipulate people into doing what you want, even if what you want is right for them, to a place where your heartfelt desire is for their best, and the person becomes better and improved because of it. Your desire shifts from being concerned with self only to being concerned with the best for the individual you are praying for. When any person improves their character they start to lose those traits and characteristics that may have been causing problems for others.

Q: I do not believe the verses given apply to me! I believe these verses are taken out of context! What should I do?

A: This question is one of the most common, but I also believe that people are trying to find a conscious reasoning to believe the truths given. Many know that there is power and truth in these prayers, but they have been taught to live in doubt, unbelief, and fear. While their faith is stirred up when praying these prayers, the underlying subconscious programming is one of doubt and defeat. That is why it is so important to say these prayers daily in affirmative faith. In doing so you eventually undo the doubt and unbelief that you do not even consciously realize is there and "reprogram" or "renew" your subconscious mind to the truths of God in Christ.

> "And be not conformed to this world: but be ye transformed by the renewing of your mind, that ye may prove what *is* that good, and acceptable, and perfect, will of God." (Romans 12:2)

The basic premise that backs all of these prayers, a premise that you must understand for successful prayer in this life, is that God "regardeth not persons" (Deuteronomy 10:17) and that with God there is no "respect of persons" (2 Chronicles 19:7; Colossians 3:25; 1 Peter 1:17; Ephesians 6:9; Romans 2:11). You must get to the place of wisdom to say like Peter did, "Of a truth I perceive that God is no respecter of persons" (Acts 10:34).

What this revelation means to you is that ANYTHING God has done for someone else He can do for you if you will simply believe. He is not holding anything back from you, if you can stand in faith believing you have received it. If a verse of Scripture is a promise of blessing or is a revelation of a blessing having been given to someone else, then you can be confident that such a blessing is also for you; if you will believe.

Q: If I do not repeatedly ask God for my desires, then won't I lessen my chance of getting my prayer answered?

A: Not at all. The idea of repeatedly asking God for the same thing is the reason why most do not get their prayers answered affirmatively. People repeatedly asking God for the same things will at times believe that their prayers were answered affirmatively due to their repetitive asking, but it is more likely to have been the result of chance, than an actual answer to prayer (see Ecclesiastes 9:11). People repeatedly ask because they feel God is not on their side and that they need to convince Him of their deserving the result that they seek. Prayer is _NOT_ a work in God's heart to get Him to come around to want to help you, rather it is you aligning yourself with His will and making yourself able to receive the thing you desire.

Imagine a man who wanted 2 gallons of water from an unlimited river, but the only container he had to hold the water in could hold merely one single gallon. He is not capable of receiving that which he desires. No matter how much he begs, pleads, and cries, he is still only able to receive one gallon of water into his vessel, even though the river's supply is infinite. The river is not refusing to give him all the water he desires, he is simply unprepared to receive it. It is the same with us and prayer. We need to convince ourselves, not God, and thus make ourselves ready to receive the blessing. You cannot receive a million-dollar blessing with a hundred-dollar mindset. That is what makes these prayers so important. You ask God for the desires of your heart and then instead of pleading with God the next day for the same thing, you prepare yourself to receive the answer by the faith-filled prayers of grateful praise and confident assurance that you have received what you asked for _when_ you prayed.

The vast majority of people have traditions and underlying subconscious programming from childhood that keeps them following certain well-worn paths. This is why we so often see children ending up in the exact same situations as their parents. They are just unconsciously following the example that they were given by parents, teachers, and people they looked up to as children. With these prayers you are patiently undoing those old programs that, unbeknownst to you, control many of your decisions and actions. This renewing of your mind is the equivalent of the man with the one-gallon container replacing that container with one that will hold the two gallons he has desired. As you pray these prayers your faith builds, and your confidence becomes sure. You will become ready to receive, and then the blessing will come.

Q: Why do I have to pray these prayers? Why can't God just give me what I need?

A: God does give you more than enough, but you may fail to receive it all. The very fact you are alive and able to consider these points is a great advantage. You have all the natural gifts and capabilities to have anything you may desire in this life, but it is up to you to become the person who can receive whatever you desire. You are where you are because life is like a mirror that reflects back the real you. If life gives you lack and want, that is because at your deepest core being you are a person of lack and want. It is part of who you have believed yourself to be and that is all you will ever be until you start making the changes needed to correct that. Daily faith-filled declarations of these prayers will start to change that inner you and renew it to the truths of who you really are in God. Once that change is made, you will then be the vessel that is able to hold all the blessings of God that once you did not even see coming to you.

> "For with the heart man believeth unto righteousness; and with the mouth confession is made unto salvation." (Romans 10:10)

Believing something and confessing it is the complete picture to get the end result desired. Just believing something alone is not enough, because "faith, if it hath not works, is dead, being alone" (James 2:17). You need to make that belief a part of your innermost being. It needs to become the real you and as true to you as your hair color or eye color. Then and only then will you be in the right state of consciousness to receive anything you should desire from the Lord.

Q: What about the widow and the unjust judge? Doesn't that prove we need to keep asking God for the same thing until He gives in?

A: This is an important section of the Scripture to deal with, so I want to first include the whole text here. Many have confused the issue of what Jesus is stating here and interpreted it as saying God will answer prayers only when badgered into answering them, which is as far from the truth as the east is from the west. Please pay careful attention to what Jesus states in this parable and the exact details given, as many people miss this and only see within the parable an excuse for unbelief and repetitive prayers. Here is the parable of the widow and the unjust judge:

Luke 18:1-8

1 And he spake a parable unto them *to this end,* that men ought always to pray, and not to faint;

2 **Saying,** There was in a city a judge, which feared not God, neither regarded man:

3 And there was a widow in that city; and she came unto him, saying, Avenge me of mine adversary.

4 And he would not for a while: but afterward he said within himself, Though I fear not God, nor regard man;

5 Yet because this widow troubleth me, I will avenge her, lest by her continual coming she weary me.

6 And the Lord said, Hear what the unjust judge saith.

7 And shall not God avenge his own elect, which cry day and night unto him, though he bear long with them?

8 I tell you that he will avenge them speedily. Nevertheless when the Son of man cometh, shall he find faith on the earth?

One of the first things to note is that Jesus is not telling you to look at an unjust judge as the example for what to expect from God in prayer. God is just, merciful, and is "the living God, who giveth us richly all things to enjoy" (1 Timothy 6:17). Jesus is showing that if an unjust judge would avenge the cause of the widow simply because she was bothering him, how much more with the great God avenge His elect! It is also important to note that this whole parable is in the context of Chapter 17 where He discussed "the day when the Son of man is revealed" (Luke 17:30). It is a parable teaching people to pray always and to not faint, but it is in the context of when the Son of man comes to earth. This is not about average prayers for things you may need or personal deliverance, rather it is about God avenging a group of people, His own elect, in the end times. Even then, Jesus does not promise a long, drawn out delay, but says, "I tell you that he will avenge them speedily" (Luke 18:8). The thought of this parable is restated later in Luke by Jesus when He says, "Watch ye therefore, and pray always, that ye may be accounted worthy to escape all these things that shall come to pass, and to stand before the Son of man" (Luke 21:36).

In regard to praying for things you may need, personal deliverance, healing, and other individual things, Jesus already plainly stated in this same book, "And I say unto you, Ask, and it shall be given you; seek, and ye shall find; knock, and it shall be opened unto you. For every one that asketh receiveth; and he that seeketh findeth; and to him that knocketh it shall be opened" (Luke 11:9-10). It is worth noting that in the context of these verses, Jesus also compared how a friend would help another simply because of the importunity (Luke 11:8), and then He compares it with God who you simply ask and receive; seek and find; and knock and it shall be opened. Jesus then continues and explains how even evil men give good gifts to their children, so how much more will God give good gifts and the Holy Spirit to them that ask Him (Luke 11:13; Matthew 7:11).

None of these passages are to indicate God shares characteristics with unjust judges or evil men, rather they are to compare and contrast the behavior of unjust and evil men who would avenge people or help in time of need when inconvenienced with the gracious and abundant action of the living God. God answers with speediness and with an overflowing abundance of the blessings which He lavishes on His children. God does not need to be persuaded, cajoled, or begged in order for the individual to get answers to their prayers.

PRAYERS:

KNOWING THE WILL OF GOD

Acts 22:14

Romans 12:2

1 Corinthians 2:16

Ephesians 5:17

God has chosen me to know His will. I have renewed my mind and continue to renew my mind daily, and know with full faith and clarity that good, acceptable, and perfect will of God. I have the mind of Christ. I am wise and understanding what the will of the Lord is.

SCHOOL

James 1:5

Proverbs 9:6

Colossians 3:23

Psalms 119:99-100

1 Timothy 4:12

God gives me great wisdom in all my studies and tests. I go in the way of understanding. All my classes and instruction are easily understandable by me, and I have tremendous knowledge in every area I choose to learn. Whatever I do, I do it heartily, as to the Lord, not unto men. I have more understanding than all my teachers: for God's testimonies are my meditation. I understand more than the ancients, because I keep God's precepts. No one despises my youth, because I am a splendid example of the believers, in word, in conversation, in charity, in spirit, in faith, and in purity.

BUSINESS

Isaiah 48:17

Deuteronomy 8:18

1 Peter 4:11

Romans 12:11

Proverbs 22:29

Ecclesiastes 9:10

Proverbs 10:4

Proverbs 13:4

James 1:5

The Lord my God teaches me to profit and leads me in the way that I should go, for it is He that gives me the power to get wealth. When I speak it is with authority as the oracles of God. I am not slothful in business, but am diligent and fervent in spirit. Whatever I choose to do, I do it with all my might and am rewarded for it bountifully with ever-expanding wealth, riches, honor, and life. God's wisdom guides my every transaction and enables me to make the right decision every time. My business is constantly expanding and blessing my customers mightily.

SUCCESS

Joshua 1:8

Romans 15:29

Philippians 4:13

Isaiah 41:10

2 Corinthians 3:18

My way is prosperous, and I have good success. Everything that I set my hand to ends up in success and blessing. I walk in the fullness of the blessing of the gospel of Christ. I can do all things through Christ which strengthens me. God is with me and strengthens me, helps me, and upholds me with the right hand of His righteousness. I go from success to success and glory to glory.

WISDOM & INTELLECT

James 1:5

Proverbs 2:6

Exodus 36:2

Exodus 31:3

Exodus 35:31

Ephesians 1:17

God gives me wisdom liberally and I am walking in His divine wisdom daily. The Lord has given me great wisdom, and knowledge, and understanding. I am a wise-hearted person whom the Lord has endued with the spirit of wisdom. The Lord has filled me with the Spirit of God, in wisdom, in understanding, and in knowledge. God has given me the Spirit of wisdom and revelation in the knowledge of Him.

HEALING

Mark 11:25-26

Exodus 15:26

Psalms 103:3

Psalms 30:2

Exodus 23:25

Jeremiah 33:6

Colossians 4:12

Proverbs 18:21

Psalms 107:20

I have forgiven anyone that has harmed me and bless them in sincerity from the love in my heart for them. God is the Lord that has healed me and keeps sickness from the midst of me. The Lord has brought me health and cure. He has cured me and revealed to me the abundance of peace and truth. I stand perfect and complete in all the will of God. Death and life are in the power of the tongue and I speak forth life and healing in my body. God sent His word and healed me, and has delivered me from my destructions.

MONEY

Proverbs 10:22

Psalms 112:3

Proverbs 15:6

Philippians 4:19

Ecclesiastes 10:19

Ecclesiastes 7:12

The blessing of the Lord has made me rich, and He adds no sorrow with it. Wealth, riches, and much treasure are in my house. My God shall supply all my need according to His riches in glory by Christ Jesus. I know that money answers all things, and God has given me a great abundance of money to answer my needs and wants, and to meet the needs and wants of others. God has blessed me with an overflowing abundance of money that provides me with a defense and protection when needed.

CREATIVITY

Proverbs 8:12

1 Corinthians 2:16

Exodus 31:3-4

Exodus 35:31-32

John 16:13

God has given and continues to give me great creativity and knowledge of witty inventions. The very infinite Mind that created the Universe and all that is therein has endowed me with the same creativity and ingenuity. I am filled with the Spirit of God, in wisdom, and in knowledge, and in understanding, and in all manner of workmanship. I can devise cunning and curious works through God's creativity that permeates my very being. The Spirit of Truth guides me into all truth and shows me things to come. I am always plentiful with creative and inspired ideas.

FORGIVENESS

Psalms 119:165

Mark 11:25

Luke 6:36-37

Matthew 5:7

Matthew 6:14

Ephesians 4:32

Colossians 3:13

Ephesians 5:2

I have great peace and nothing shall offend me. As I pray I have forgiven anyone I have ought or a grievance with. I am merciful and forgiving to all people, even as my Father is merciful and forgiving to me. I do not hold any unforgiveness toward anyone. I walk in love, as Christ has loved me, and I always see the good and honorable things in all people, and presume the best about them.

PEACE

Job 22:21

Job 34:29

Isaiah 30:15

1 Corinthians 14:33

Psalm 119:165

Isaiah 26:3

2 Corinthians 13:11

1 Samuel 25:6

I have acquainted myself with God and am at peace, thereby good shall come to me. God has given me quietness, who then can make trouble? In quietness and confidence, I have strength. God is not the author of confusion, but of peace. God keeps me in perfect peace, because my mind is stayed on Him, and I trust in Him. The God of love and peace is with me. Peace is with me, peace is in my house, and peace is in all that I have.

ANXIETY & WORRY

Philippians 4:6-7

1 Peter 5:7

2 Peter 1:4

Luke 17:21

Romans 14:17

Isaiah 43:5

I am anxious for nothing. The peace of God, which passes all understanding, keeps my heart and mind through Christ Jesus. I have cast all my care upon God, and He cares for me and puts me in perfect unity with His divine nature. The Kingdom of God is within me and I am overflowing with righteousness, peace, and joy in the Holy Ghost. I have no anxiety, worry, or fear, for God is with me.

FEAR

2 Timothy 1:7

Psalms 23:4

1 John 4:18

Job 11:15

Luke 8:50

God has not given me the spirit of fear; but of power, and of love, and of a sound mind. I fear no evil, because God is with me. There is no fear in love, and I am walking in God's perfect love which casts out ALL fear. I lift up my face without spot or shame, and am steadfast and fearless. I walk without fear and believe only.

<u>SLEEP</u>

Proverbs 3:24

Psalms 3:5

Psalms 4:8

Leviticus 26:6

Job 11:18-19

Psalms 127:2

Jeremiah 31:26

Isaiah 40:31

I lay down in peace and my sleep is sweet. I awake refreshed and energized because the Lord sustained me. I sleep in the perfect safety of God. I am His beloved and He gives me refreshing and renewing sleep. I sleep in full trust in the Lord, waiting on Him, and awake renewed in my spirit, soul, mind, and body. I shall mount up with wings as eagles; I shall run, and not be weary; and I shall walk, and not faint.

CONFIDENCE

Proverbs 28:1

Psalms 27:1

Ephesians 3:16

Philippians 4:13

Proverbs 3:26

John 15:5

2 Corinthians 3:5

I am bold as a lion. The LORD is my light and my salvation; whom shall I fear? The LORD is the strength of my life; of whom shall I be afraid? I am strengthened with might by His Spirit in my inner man. I can do all things through Christ which strengthens me. The Lord is my confidence. I abide in Christ, and He abides in me, and I bring forth much fruit because my sufficiency is of God.

PROTECTION

Psalms 91:9-10

Psalms 121:7

Proverbs 12:21

Job 5:19

Psalms 121:8

Isaiah 43:2

No evil shall befall me, neither shall any plague come nigh my dwelling. God gives His angels charge over me, to keep and protect me in all my ways. The Lord preserves me from evil and preserves my soul. No evil shall happen to me. God shall deliver me in six troubles, even in seven shall no evil touch me. Wherever I go and whatever I go through, God is with me and protects me. The Lord preserves and protects my going out and my coming in now and forevermore.

FEELING INSIGNIFICANT OR INFERIOR

Psalms 82:6

Acts 17:28

Genesis 1:26-27

2 Corinthians 6:16-18

Luke 17:21

2 Peter 1:4

I am a child of the most High! I live, and move, and have my being in God, because I am His offspring. I am created in the image and likeness of the Almighty. God is my Father and dwells in me, walks in me, and is my God, and I am his child. The kingdom of God is within me and I am a partaker of the divine nature.

MARRIAGE (FOR MEN)

Proverbs 18:22

Proverbs 5:18-19

Ecclesiastes 9:9

Proverbs 19:14

Proverbs 31:10-31

1 Peter 3:4

Ephesians 5:25

I have found a good thing by finding my wife, and have obtained the favor of the Lord. I rejoice with the wife of my youth, and am satisfied with her and always ravished with her love. I live joyfully with my wife, whom I love all the days of my life. My wife is prudent and virtuous and is a blessing from the Lord. My heart does safely trust in my wife, because she does me good and not evil all the days of her life. Strength and honor are my wife's clothing, and her adornment is a meek and quiet spirit. My wife opens her mouth with wisdom, and in her tongue is the law of kindness. My wife is blessed and I love her as Christ loves the Church.

MARRIAGE (FOR WOMEN)

1 Peter 3:2

Ephesians 5:25, 28, 33

Colossians 3:19

1 Peter 3:7

Proverbs 31:28

Song of Solomon 7:10

My husband beholds my chaste and dignified behavior. My husband loves me even as himself, even as his own body. My husband is so in love with me that he loves me even as Christ loved the Church, and gave Himself for it. My husband loves me and is not bitter towards me. My husband is tender and sweet to me, and gives me honor and praise. I am my beloved's, and his desire is only toward me.

CHILDREN

Acts 16:31

Isaiah 54:13

John 3:16

Psalms 37:23

Romans 2:4

Romans 11:22

Joshua 24:15

I have believed on Jesus and me and my house shall be saved. All of my children are taught of the LORD, and great is the peace of my children. I release my son/daughter/children to God. God loves and cares for my son/daughter/children. He is leading and guiding them every step of the way. The goodness of God prevails in my son/daughter's life. As for me and my house, we will serve the Lord.

LEGAL ISSUES

Isaiah 49:25

Psalms 5:12

Psalms 28:7

Psalms 46:1

Psalms 138:7

Isaiah 54:17

Proverbs 3:4

God will contend with those people who contend with me. God encompasses me with favor as with a shield. The Lord is my strength and my shield; my heart trusted in Him, and I am helped. God is my refuge and strength, a very present help in trouble. Though I walk in the midst of trouble, Lord God you will revive me: you will stretch forth your hand against the wrath of my enemies and your right hand shall save me. No weapon that is formed against me shall prosper; and every tongue that shall rise against me in judgment shall be condemned. I have favor and good understanding in the sight of God and man, and will have an outcome that is favorable to me.

ADDICTION

Romans 13:11-13

1 Peter 5:8

John 8:36

Ephesians 5:18

Galatians 5:21-24

I have cast off the works of darkness and have put on the armor of light. I walk honestly, as in the day, with soberness of mind and heart. I have given up addiction and walk in freedom and grace. The Son has made me free and I am free indeed. I have chosen to not get drunk or high, instead I have chosen to be filled with the Spirit. I have crucified the flesh with the affections and lusts and walk in love, joy, peace, longsuffering, gentleness, goodness, faith, meekness, and temperance.

NEGATIVITY

Isaiah 26:3

1 John 4:16

Philippians 4:8

1 Thessalonians 4:9

1 John 3:23

1 Peter 4:8

My mind is stayed on God, Who is love. I only allow thoughts that are true, honest, just, pure, lovely, of good report, virtuous, and praiseworthy. I am taught of God to love others, and negativity would be contrary to my nature of divine love.

COMMUNICATION

Proverbs 25:11

Proverbs 16:24

1 Peter 4:11

Colossians 4:6

Ephesians 4:29

All my words are fitly spoken and are like apples of gold in pictures of silver. My words are pleasant and sweet to the soul and health to the bones. I speak boldly and with authority, as the oracles of God. My speech is always with grace and I know how to answer every person. No corrupt communication proceeds from my mouth, rather my communication is only good to the use of edifying, that it may minister grace unto the hearers.

THANKSGIVING
&
GRATEFULNESS

Psalms 69:30

Colossians 2:7

Jeremiah 30:19

Psalms 107:1

Psalms 106:1

Psalms 118:1

Psalms 136:1

2 Corinthians 2:14

Ephesians 5:20

I magnify God with thanksgiving. I am abounding in thanksgiving and out of me proceeds thanksgiving and gratefulness. I give thanks unto the Lord, for He is good and His mercy endures forever. Now thanks be unto God, which always causes me to triumph in Christ. I give thanks always for all things unto God and the Father in the name of my Lord Jesus Christ.

RELATIONSHIPS

Hebrews 10:24

Ephesians 4:1-3

Proverbs 17:17

Proverbs 18:24

In all my relationships we encourage one another to be loving and do good works. I walk worthy of the vocation wherewith I was called, with all humility, meekness, longsuffering, and loving patience with others. I endeavor to keep the unity of the Spirit in the bond of peace, and those I associate with follow my loving lead. I have friends that love me at all times and I show myself friendly and loving towards them.

BODY IMAGE

2 Corinthians 6:19-20

Romans 12:1

Psalms 100:3

Isaiah 44:2

Psalms 119:68

James 1:17

I am the temple of the Holy Ghost. I glorify God in my body and in my spirit. My body is holy and acceptable unto God. God has made me and formed me from the womb. Everything God makes is good, and I am good. I am a good and perfect gift to the world that came from the Father of lights.

PROSPERITY

Proverbs 10:22

Deuteronomy 8:18

Isaiah 48:17

Psalms 112:3

Proverbs 15:6

Proverbs 3:16

Psalms 68:19

The blessing of the Lord has made me rich, and He adds NO sorrow with it. It is the Lord who has given me the power to get wealth, and Who teaches me to profit. Wealth and riches and much treasure are in my house, and my righteousness endures forever. Riches and honor are mine. Blessed be the Lord, Who daily loads me with benefits!

ABUNDANCE

Job 22:24

Proverbs 21:5

John 10:10

Matthew 13:12

Ephesians 3:20

2 Corinthians 9:8

I have such abundance that I can lay up gold with such plenteousness as dust and as the stones of the brooks. My thoughts tend only to plenteousness, and visions of divine abundance are ever before me. Jesus came that I might have life, and that I might have it more abundantly, and I live that abundant life each and every day. I am abundantly blessed and will have even more abundance. God does exceeding abundantly above all that I ask or think, according to the power that works in me. I have all sufficiency in all things and abound to every good work.

PROMOTION

Psalms 75:6-7

Proverbs 3:16

Proverbs 4:8

John 15:16

My promotion does not come from anyone but God, Who chose to raise me up in His glory. Because God has graced me with His infinite wisdom I am promoted and brought to honor and esteem. I am chosen and ordained to bring forth fruit, and my fruit shall remain.

LACK AND WANT

Proverbs 34:9-10

1 Thessalonians 4:11-12

Psalms 23:1

Philippians 4:19

Romans 8:32

1 Corinthians 3:21-22

Psalms 84:11

There is no want or lack to me, because those that seek the LORD shall not want ANY good thing. I am diligent in my business and lack nothing. The Lord is my shepherd and I shall not want. God supplies all my need according to His riches in glory by Christ Jesus. God freely gives me all things, and all things are mine. The Lord God is a sun and shield for me, He gives me grace and glory, and He withholds no good thing from me.

GOVERNMENT

Romans 13:4

1 Timothy 2:1-2

1 Peter 2:17

Acts 23:5

Ecclesiastes 10:20

Exodus 22:28

Jude 8

I am thankful for the rulers who are ministers of God to me for good. I pray for all men, including those in authority, and I lead a quiet and peaceable life in all godliness and honesty. I pray for those in government to have the wisdom from God to make decisions for good and peace. I honor those in leadership and only speak good, uplifting, and edifying words about them.

MINDSET

Romans 12:1

Ephesians 1:18

2 Corinthians 4:6

1 Corinthians 2:16

Ephesians 4:23-24

2 Corinthians 10:5

My mind is renewed and proves what is that good, acceptable, and perfect will of God. The eyes of my understanding are enlightened by the light of the knowledge of the glory of God in the face of Jesus Christ. I have the mind of Christ and His infinite intelligence is available to me at any moment I so desire. I am renewed in the spirit of my mind and have put on the new man, which after God is created in righteousness and true holiness. I cast down imaginations, and every high thing that exalts itself against the knowledge of God, and bring into captivity every thought to the obedience of Christ.

EVERY DAY IS A GOOD DAY

Psalms 118:24

Psalms 121:7

Numbers 6:24-26

Psalms 23:6

This is the day that the Lord has made, I will rejoice and be glad in it. The Lord preserves me from all evil and preserves my soul. The Lord blesses me and keeps me. The Lord makes His face to shine upon me, and is gracious unto me. The Lord lifts up His countenance upon me and gives me peace. Surely goodness and mercy follow me all the days of my life. I walk in the peace, prosperity, riches, wealth, abundance, health, favor, wisdom, and joy of the Lord.

JOY

Romans 15:13

Romans 14:17

Luke 17:21

Psalms 43:4

Psalms 16:11

The God of hope has filled me with all joy and peace in believing. The kingdom of God is righteousness, peace, and joy in the Holy Ghost, and the kingdom of God is within me! God is my exceeding joy and I am in His presence where there is fullness of joy.

VICTORY

1 John 4:4

1 Corinthians 15:57

Romans 8:37

2 Corinthians 2:14

1 John 5:4

Greater is He that is in me than he that is in the world. Thanks be to God, which gives me the victory through my Lord Jesus Christ. I am more than a conqueror through Him that loves me. Thanks be unto God, which always causes me to triumph in Christ. I overcome the world and get the victory in all things by my faith.

SAFETY

Proverbs 21:31

Psalms 3:3

Proverbs 3:23

Psalms 4:8

Job 11:18

Isaiah 54:17

Safety is of the Lord, and He keeps me safe in every way. O Lord, you are a shield for me; my glory, and the lifter of my head. God makes me dwell in safety. I walk in my way safely, and my foot shall not stumble. I am secure in Him and I take my rest in safety. No weapon that is formed against me shall prosper; and every tongue that shall rise against me in judgment shall be condemned.

ENEMIES

Luke 1:74-75

Matthew 5:44

1 Peter 3:9

Romans 12:21

God has delivered me out of the hand of my enemies and I serve Him without fear, in holiness and righteousness before Him, all the days of my life. I love my enemies, I bless those that curse me, I do good to them that hate me, and I pray for those which despitefully use me and persecute me. I am not overcome with evil, but overcome evil with good.

BLESSING FOR THE HOME

Job 5:24

Psalms 112:3

Psalms 101:2

Proverbs 15:6

Proverbs 21:20

Proverbs 24:3-4

My home is in peace, and I shall visit my habitation and shall not sin. Wealth and riches are in my house, and my righteousness endures forever. I will walk within my house with a perfect heart. In my house is much treasure and desirable things. My house is built by wisdom, established by understanding, and by knowledge each room is filled with all precious and pleasant riches.

WEAKNESS

Joel 3:10

2 Samuel 22:33

Psalms 18:32

Psalms 27:1

2 Corinthians 12:9

Philippians 4:13

I am strong and have overcome weakness. God is my strength and power: and He makes my way perfect. The Lord is the strength of my life; of whom shall I be afraid? God's grace is sufficient for me, for His strength is made perfect in weakness. I can do all things through Christ which strengthens me.

PETS

Proverbs 12:10

Genesis 1:20-26

Matthew 10:29

Luke 12:6, 24

James 1:5

I am grateful for my pet and I am kind and compassionate toward them. My pet is the way that God created them to be and is good. God watches over my pet and cares for them. I thank God for the understanding and wisdom to interact with my pet in a way that best blesses both them and me.

<u>FINANCE</u>

Proverbs 10:22

James 1:5

Proverbs 10:4

Proverbs 13:11

Psalms 23:1

Philippians 4:19

The blessing of the Lord has made me rich, and He adds no sorrow with it. God gives me wisdom in all my financial endeavors. I gain wealth by my diligent labor and I steadily increase each day in my financial prosperity. I have no financial lack or want, because the Lord is my shepherd and supplies all my need by His riches in glory by Christ Jesus.

REAL ESTATE

Deuteronomy 1:8; 3:18; 4:22

1 Chronicles 28:8

God has given me my good land and I am blessed in possessing it. I possess the good land, and leave it for my children after me forever.

CLOSING COMMENTS

I do not want you to feel that you are alone, especially if some of this is new to you. I welcome you to contact me if you are struggling or need help in getting the results you are desiring. You can contact me at coaching@taughttoprofit.com.

I also would welcome you to send testimonials from your experience praying these prayers. I will be adding testimonials periodically to the book as it goes through updates and revisions. These testimonials can build your faith when telling them and be a helpful blessing to others who may be wavering in their faith.

"Beloved, I wish above all things that thou mayest prosper and be in health, even as thy soul prospereth." (3 John 2)

"Every good gift and every perfect gift is from above, and cometh down from the Father of lights, with whom is no variableness, neither shadow of turning." (James 1:17)

About Ryan Hicks:

http://www.TaughtToProfit.com

God has blessed Ryan with a wide variety of investments, including Forex, stocks, options, real estate, cryptocurrency, physical businesses, and online businesses. By the age of 23, he had built his first multi-million-dollar company. He strives to help people achieve success themselves through their own businesses and investments. He is passionate about helping people break out of the limiting mindsets that keep them from attaining the success, joy, and peace they deserve. His website is: TaughtToProfit.com

www.ingramcontent.com/pod-product-compliance
Lightning Source LLC
Chambersburg PA
CBHW031332040426
42443CB00005B/308